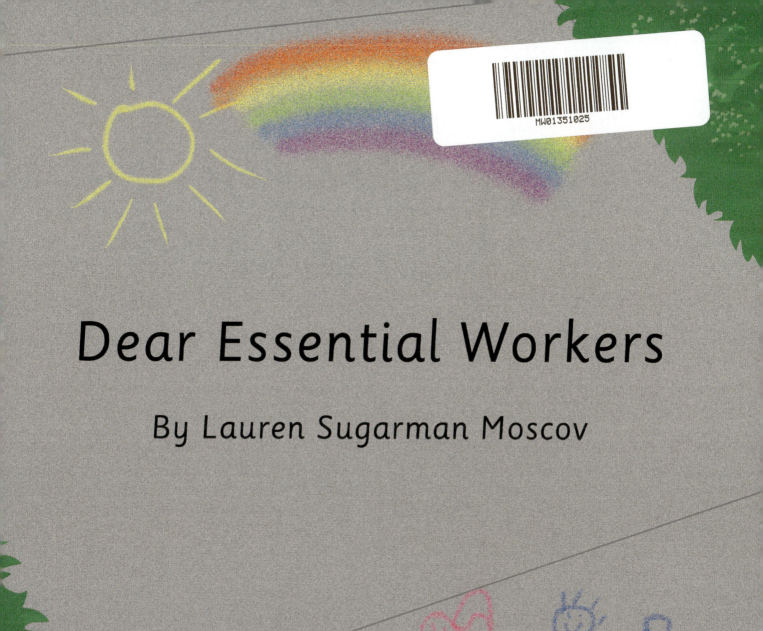

Dear Essential Workers

By Lauren Sugarman Moscov

First and foremost, this book is dedicated to essential workers as a small token of my deep gratitude. 100 percent of the proceeds from sales of these books will go to COVID-19 research and relief efforts.

This book is also dedicated to my children: Jack, Ivy and Ari. Never underestimate the power of a heartfelt "thank you."
Thank you each for inspiring me to be better and show you better.
I love you!

Dear Essential Workers
All Rights Reserved
Copyright © 2020 Lauren Sugarman Moscov

This book may not be reproduced, transmitted, or stored in whole or part by any means, including graphic, electronic, or mechanical without the express written consent of the author except in the case of brief quotations embodied in critical articles or reviews.

Cover & Interior images © 2020 Lauren Sugarman Moscov.
All rights reserved.

Illustrated by Stacy Hummel

Thank you, Essential Workers

When a new virus came on the scene,
A lot changed due to COVID 19.
It was no longer safe to be out and about.
"Shelter in place," the experts did shout.
As we stay home to learn, work and play
A group of workers go out of their way
To make sure we get our supplies,
Like food and water; sometimes a surprise.
This book is a BIG thank-you note
To all those who keep us afloat.

Thank You, Grocery Store Workers

Workers at corner, grocery, and super stores
Put on gloves and masks as they walk through the doors,
To keep shelves stocked with food and supplies,
So we can cook, bake, clean and sterilize.
As you eat your breakfast or feed your dog, Frank,
It's grocery store workers who you should thank.

Thank You,
Postal Service and Delivery Drivers

In cars, bikes, vans and trucks,
Delivery drivers make sure we're not stuck
Without the items we want and need,
Like letters, puzzles and books to read.
For all the boxes they leave by the door,
It's delivery drivers whom we all adore.

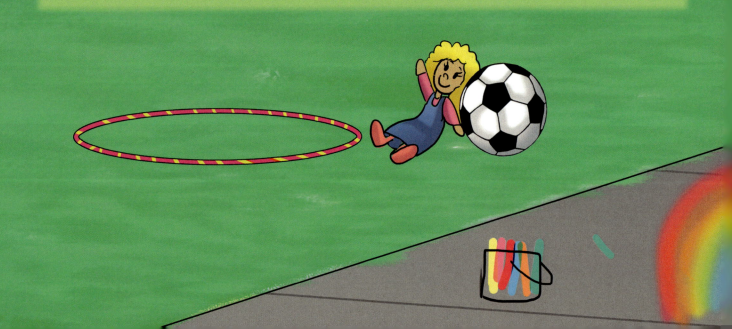

Thank You, Healthcare Workers

Doctors, nurses and technicians
Pharmacists, janitors and clinicians.
They heal patients, clean spaces
Offer comfort and friendly faces.
They work so hard and take on risk
To help those who've fallen sick.
Each day, they put themselves in danger
Always willing to help a stranger.
Everyday lives they save
A noble road they do pave.
To offices, pharmacies and hospitals they go.
Make sure to thank a medical hero.

Thank you,
Field Workers, Ranchers and Farmers

They grow the food that we eat
Vegetables, fruit, grains and meat.
The hours are long, and the work is tough,
Ensuring Americans have enough
Of foods that help us move and grow.
To field workers, ranchers and farmers, our thanks we owe.

Thank You, Restaurant Workers

When a special meal is what you want
You call up the local restaurant.
And in just a short while,
Your food is delivered with a smile.
Hamburgers, pizza, even a cake
Whatever you crave they will make.
To workers at restaurants and cafes
Thank-you, is what we say.

Thank you, First Responders

When someone is hurt or in trouble,
First responders are there, on the double
To stop a fire or save a life,
Amid the chaos, danger and strife
When there is an emergency, dial 911,
And to the problem they will run.
Paramedics, police and fire departments
Protect offices, homes and apartments.
The help they give is no small favor.
In our appreciation we never waiver

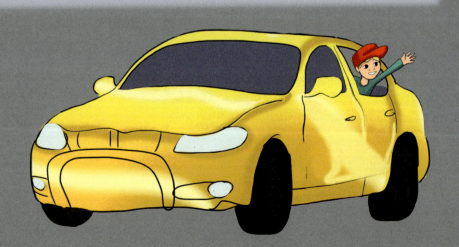

Thank You,
Teachers and Childcare Workers

Teaching kids math and helping them read,
Shaping young minds, deserves thanks, indeed.

Teachers help us to become our best.
When school buildings closed, they were put to the test. As our classrooms moved to cyber space,
They adapted with speed, dedication and grace.
Still inspiring the imagination,
Encouraging discovery and creation.
While school might not be the same as it was,
It's teachers who make learning buzz.
We're grateful for all that teachers do
From the bottom of our hearts, we say, "Thank-you."

Thank You,
Sanitation and Utility Workers

They empty trash cans along the street
Help make buildings clean and neat.
Ensuring our homes have water and power
Fixing a problem no matter the hour.
In big trucks, they clatter by,
before the sun tops the sky.
Helping towns function is what they do.
Sanitation and utility workers, we thank- you.

Thank You, Factory Workers

Working hard in the factories, you will find,
Operators of machines that crank and grind.
To make the things we use each day,
Toilet paper, masks, and sanitizing spray.
The machines can be dangerous, the factories loud,
Of these hard-working folks we all feel so proud.
To the factory workers punching the clock,
Thank you for being our country's rock.

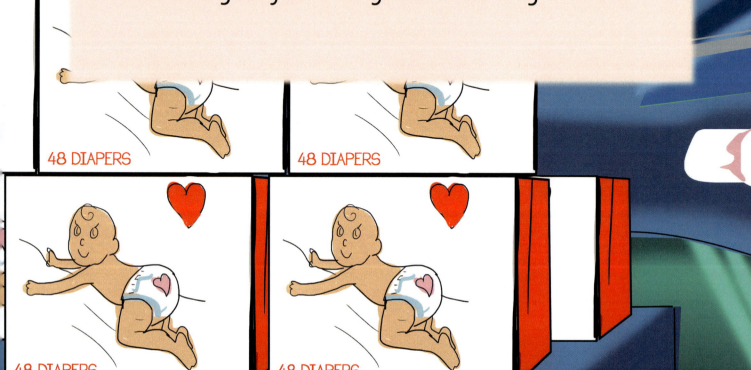

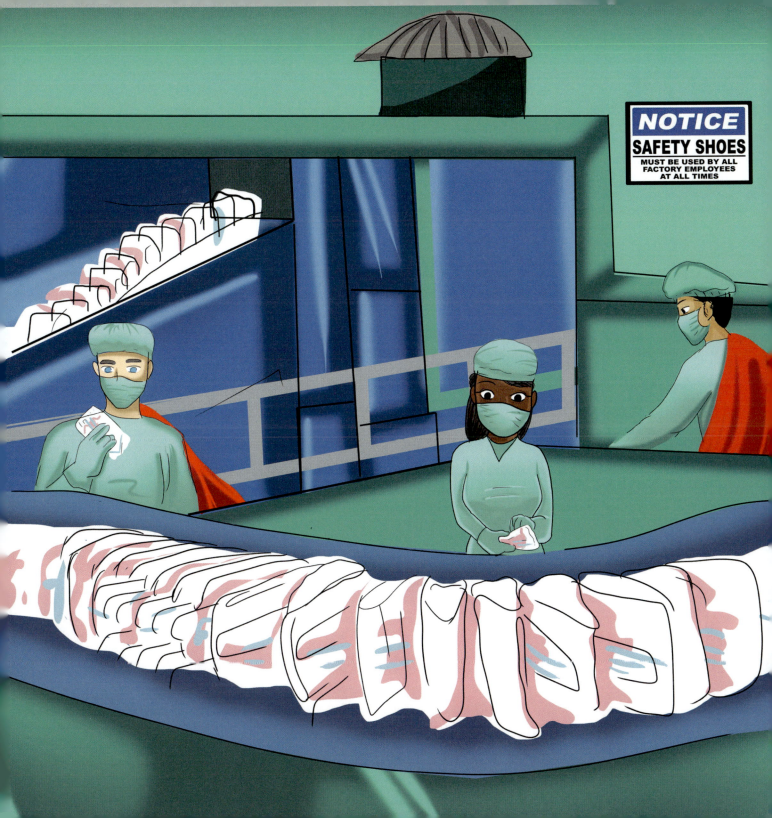

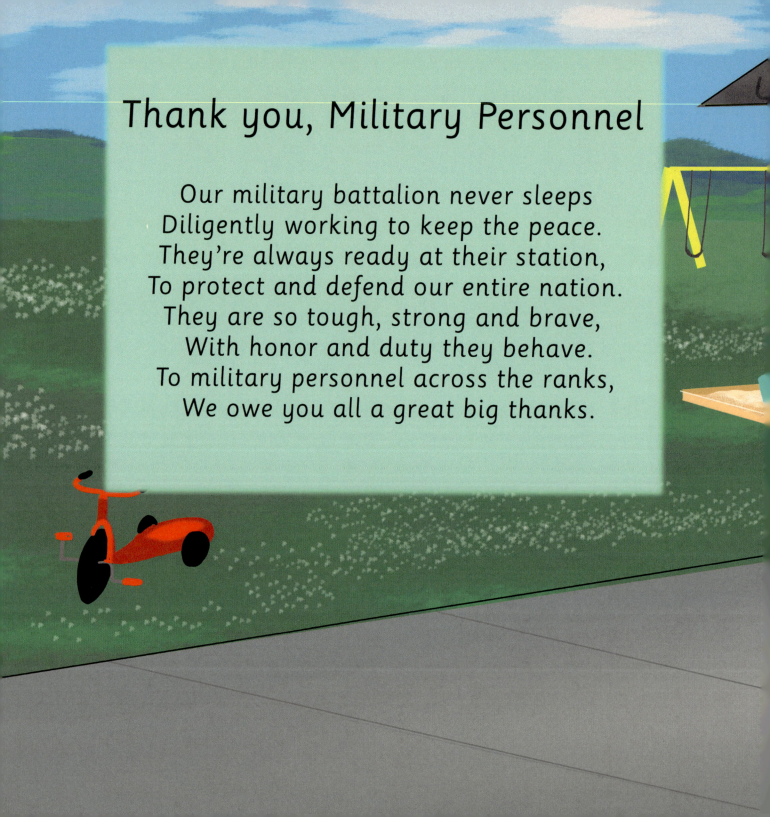

Thank you, Military Personnel

Our military battalion never sleeps
Diligently working to keep the peace.
They're always ready at their station,
To protect and defend our entire nation.
They are so tough, strong and brave,
With honor and duty they behave.
To military personnel across the ranks,
We owe you all a great big thanks.

Thank you,
Clergy and Community Leaders

To the leaders of groups who could no longer gather,
Those who guide us up the spiritual ladder.
They find new ways to keep us connected
And resources for those being affected.
Providing faith or a new perspective,
Like how to be of service to the collective.
Answering tough questions and giving us hope,
Reminding us all we have the strength to cope.
To clergy and community leaders,
Accept this thanks on behalf of all readers.

Thank You, Kids

While kids are not on the front line,
You've been acting mighty fine.
Dealing with all this change,
Some that's fun, some that's strange.
You took this time to be wiser and kinder
Giving grown ups a good reminder.
With all the worry over new changes and rules,
You carry on and keep your cool.
So I say to you, dear reader,
Thank you for being a wonderful leader.

Discussion Guide for Families

- Why do you think the author wrote this book?

- What are some of the jobs of essential workers?

- How do those jobs help us?

- Do you know any essential workers?

- Is there something we could do to say thank you to the essential workers we know?

- Who are some other essential workers in our community?

- Is there something we could do to say thank you to them?
- How can you be a helper?

Kids Activities to Thank Essential Workers

*Essential Workers Rock! Collect rocks and paint them with messages of thanks to place near the homes and businesses of essential workers.

*Give Them a (Snack) Break! Decorate lunch bags with kind words and fill them with healthy, protein-packed snacks to deliver to local hospitals and other places of business where essential workers log long hours.

*Note Your Thanks! Use this template to write a thank you note to pass along to an essential worker in your community.

> Dear (insert worker's name),
>
> Thank you for keeping us safe and healthy. I am grateful to you for helping to (insert how their job helps).
>
> Love,
>
> Child's Name

Thank you

Made in the USA
Columbia, SC
22 November 2020